m

DISCOVER●SCIENCE
FLIGHT

Kim Taylor

Chrysalis Children's Books

DISCOVER SCIENCE

Contents

This edition published in 2003 by
Chrysalis Children's Books
64 Brewery Road, London N7 9NT

Copyright © Chrysalis Books PLC
Text © Kim Taylor Times Four Publishing Ltd
Photographs © Kim Taylor and Jane Burton
(except where credited elsewhere)

A Belitha Book

British Library Cataloguing in Publication Data: CIP data
for this book is available from the British Library.

ISBN 1 84138 617 0

Designed by Tony Potter, Times Four Publishing Ltd
Illustrated by Chris Lyon
Science writer/adviser: Susan Mcmillan, BBC Natural
History Unit, Bristol
Science adviser: Richard Oels, Warden Park School,
Cuckfield, Sussex

Origination by Bright Arts, Hong Kong

Typeset by Amber Graphics, Burgess Hill

Printed in Hong Kong

About this book

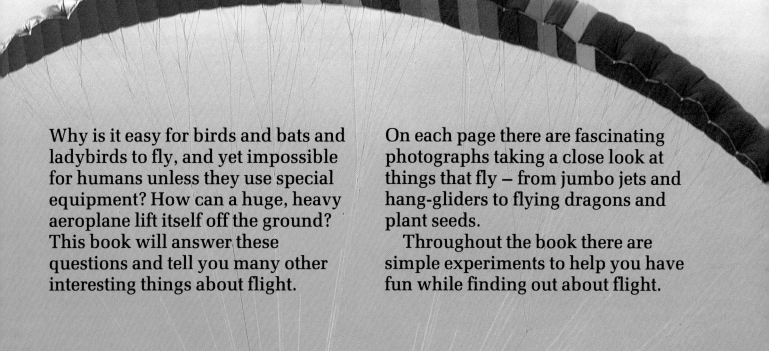

Why is it easy for birds and bats and ladybirds to fly, and yet impossible for humans unless they use special equipment? How can a huge, heavy aeroplane lift itself off the ground? This book will answer these questions and tell you many other interesting things about flight.

On each page there are fascinating photographs taking a close look at things that fly – from jumbo jets and hang-gliders to flying dragons and plant seeds.

Throughout the book there are simple experiments to help you have fun while finding out about flight.

Flying

There is a force called **gravity** that surrounds the Earth and pulls everything downwards. If you throw something into the air, gravity makes it fall back to the ground. Anything that flies has to overcome gravity.

Most birds and many insects can fly because they have wings that work in the air, lifting them up. Aeroplanes can fly because they also have wings that produce **lift**. Gliders and hang-gliders fly in a similar way, although they do not have engines to move them forward.

People cannot overcome gravity for more than a few seconds. Even the best athletes can jump no further forward than about 8 metres before gravity pulls them back to the ground. To fly, people have to use some kind of aircraft.

Bird power

Large birds, like this gannet, have huge chest muscles. They use them to power their wings.

Hummingbird

The hummingbird **hovers** in the air so it can sip **nectar** from flowers with its long beak and tongue.

Lift

All aeroplane wings are a similar shape, called an **aerofoil**. A slice taken through a wing shows that it is curved on top and flat underneath. When the wing moves forwards, the air rushes past, but it has to travel further over the top of the wing than underneath it. Because of this, the air on top of the wing is 'stretched',

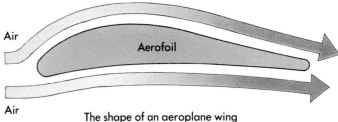

The shape of an aeroplane wing

which means that it is at a lower pressure than the air underneath. The difference in air pressure above and below the wing pushes the wing up, causing the aeroplane to rise. This effect is known as lift.

Jet aeroplanes have powerful engines that move them through the air fast. Air rushing over the wings provides the lift that keeps the plane in the air.

Freefall

To freefall is to fall through the air without opening a parachute or using any other flying equipment. When a person, or an animal, falls from a height, their speed through the air increases as they fall. Then, as they fall faster, the air pushes against them. When the force of gravity that pulls them down is balanced by **air resistance** that slows them, they stop going any faster and fall at a steady speed. Freefalling people reach a maximum speed of around 190 km/h.

By using the force of the air pushing against their bodies, these freefallers can steer themselves into position.

Freefalling for fun

People freefall from planes from heights of over 5000 metres. Their fall is slowed by the air pushing against them. At the last minute, they open their **parachutes**.

Squirrels

Squirrels can leap through the air and land without hurting themselves because they are so light, and the air pushing against them slows their fall.

They use their bushy tails to guide themselves through the air.

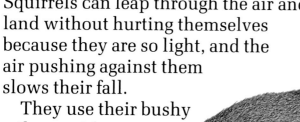

Did you know?

In July 1988, 144 US freefall parachutists joined hands to form a huge diamond shape as they fell through the air.

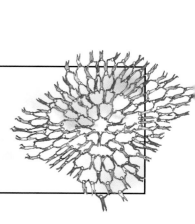

Stopping a 'cat'astrophic fall

Why does a cat always land on its feet when it falls? Because it can turn itself the right way up in mid-air. As it falls, it twists: first its head, next the front of its body and then the back. Finally, it stretches its legs out and arches its back before making a perfect landing.

Flight experiment

LIGHT AS A FEATHERED POTATO!

You need
- 2 equal-sized potatoes
- 2 large, stiff wing feathers

This experiment shows how air resistance slows down objects as they fall through the air.

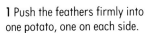

1 Push the feathers firmly into one potato, one on each side.

2 Drop both potatoes from a high place.

3 Which potato takes longer to reach the ground?

The potato with the feathers is slower, because the feathers increase the air resistance and slow it down.

Parachutes

A parachute acts as an air brake, catching the air and slowing the fall of the parachutist. People use parachutes for sport and also to save lives when jumping from crashing planes.

Some plant seeds use their own parachutes to float through the air, blown by the wind. In this way they travel great distances into new areas where they can grow. Drifting away on the wind helps to spread the plants and prevents overcrowding.

Seed parachutes

The seeds of some plants are shaped like parachutes. This light, feathery goatsbeard seed catches the air and floats away to find a new area to grow in.

Parachutes for people

Man-made parachutes are made of very light material and are connected by ropes and straps to a harness worn round the body. Some parachutes can be steered by pulling on the straps. Experienced parachutists can jump from thousands of metres up and land on a small target.

Flight experiment

PLASTICINE PARACHUTIST

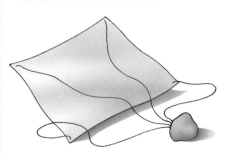

1 Tie a length of string to each corner of the handkerchief (or piece of plastic).

2 Make sure all the strings are the same length.

3 Attach about 50 g of Plasticine to the loose ends of the strings.

4 Holding the centre of the handkerchief or plastic, throw the parachute up into the air. The air should catch in the parachute and bring it floating to the ground.

If it plummets to the ground, try using less Plasticine. It may also work better if you make a small hole in the top of the parachute.

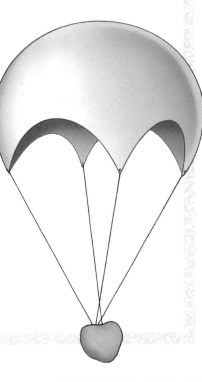

Did you know?

Spiders with gossamer 'parachutes' have been found at a height of 8000 metres – almost as high as Mt Everest!

Parachuting spiders

Some small spiders can travel 30 km, blown by the wind. This spider flight is called 'ballooning', but it is actually a form of parachuting.

The spiders' silken threads catch the wind in much the same way as man-made parachutes do.

Parascending

Rather than using parachutes to slow their fall, some people use them to rise into the air. One way of doing this is for the parachutist to be pulled along by boat or car so that the parachute acts as a wing, creating lift.

9

Gliders

There are some unexpected creatures that move quite long distances through the air – creatures such as frogs, snakes, lizards and even fish!

They use flaps of skin (rather like a parachute) or special fins to catch the air and stop them from falling too fast. But, unlike parachuting seeds and spiders, these creatures do not just move downwards. They also move forwards through the air in a controlled way. This is called gliding.

Water wings

Flying fish build up speed under water and leap out into the air. They then hold their fins rigid like wings and glide for quite long distances at speeds of up to 40 km/ph.

Flying fur

Flying squirrels and sugar gliders glide from one tree to another in search of food and also to escape from **predators**.

Their 'wings' are flaps of fur-covered skin stretched between their front and back legs.

This sugar glider is like a flying possum. It lives in Australia.

Did you know?

The highest a glider has so far reached is just under 15,000 metres.

Flying dragons

This flying dragon from Indonesia is really a lizard. It has ribs covered in scaly skin that stick out from its body. These form wings that allow it to glide through the air. At rest, the lizard folds its ribs against its body.

Kites

Kites are like gliders, but a string stops them from getting away. Like the flying dragon, a kite has large flat areas to catch the air. The wind rushing over the kite gives it lift.

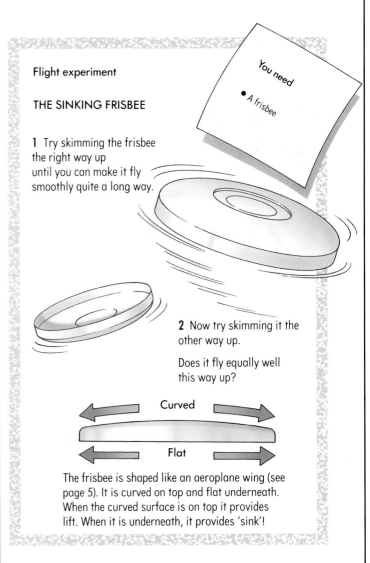

Flight experiment

THE SINKING FRISBEE

You need
• A frisbee

1 Try skimming the frisbee the right way up until you can make it fly smoothly quite a long way.

2 Now try skimming it the other way up.

Does it fly equally well this way up?

Curved

Flat

The frisbee is shaped like an aeroplane wing (see page 5). It is curved on top and flat underneath. When the curved surface is on top it provides lift. When it is underneath, it provides 'sink'!

11

Insect wings

Flying insects first appeared on Earth about 270 million years ago. Some of these insects were rather like dragonflies and had a **wingspan** of 60 cm. Imagine one of those flying over your pond!

Insects fly by flapping or buzzing their wings, although dragonflies and butterflies can also glide.

A large insect, such as a butterfly, flaps its wings about 5 to 12 times per second. Small insects have to beat their wings much more quickly.

Rigid wings

Some insects, such as ladybirds, have hard front wings which, when folded up, form wing cases to protect the back wings. When the insect flies its wing cases are held out of the way.

On the wing

When this hornet flies, it beats its wings up and down while at the same time twisting them at the base. The beating wings draw air from above and in front and pull it backwards and downwards, supporting the weight of the hornet and driving it forwards.

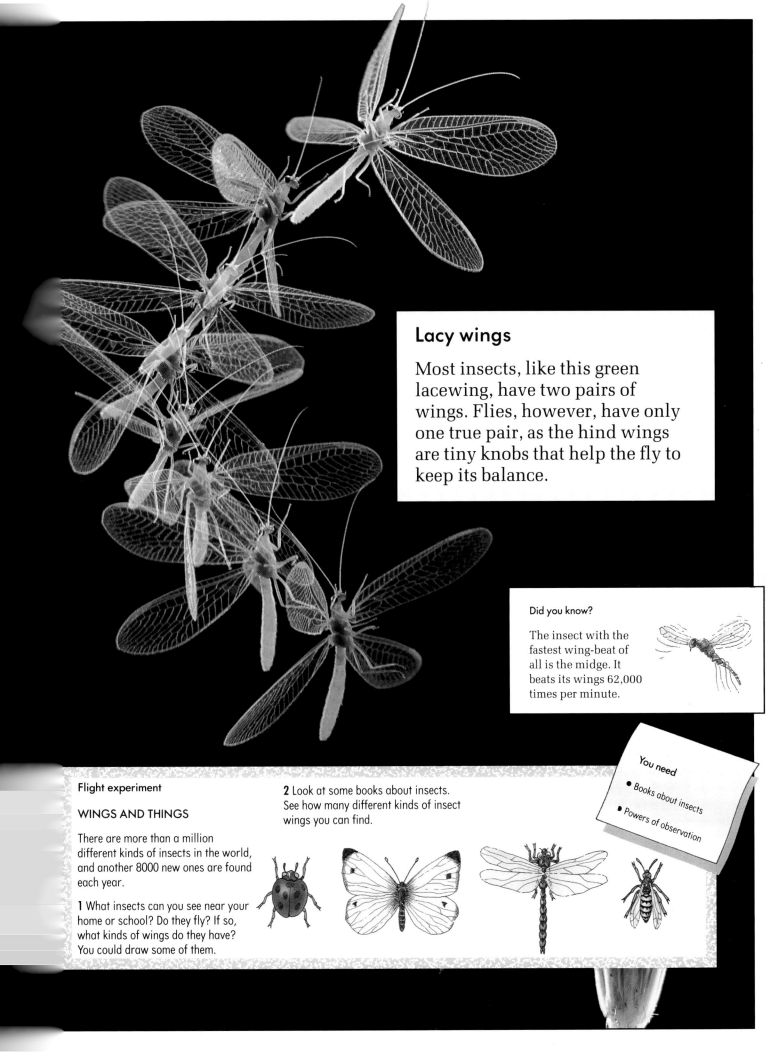

Lacy wings

Most insects, like this green lacewing, have two pairs of wings. Flies, however, have only one true pair, as the hind wings are tiny knobs that help the fly to keep its balance.

Did you know?

The insect with the fastest wing-beat of all is the midge. It beats its wings 62,000 times per minute.

You need
- Books about insects
- Powers of observation

Flight experiment

WINGS AND THINGS

There are more than a million different kinds of insects in the world, and another 8000 new ones are found each year.

1 What insects can you see near your home or school? Do they fly? If so, what kinds of wings do they have? You could draw some of them.

2 Look at some books about insects. See how many different kinds of insect wings you can find.

Flapping wings

Birds are nature's supreme fliers, and they are perfectly designed for flight. They are strongly but lightly built, with hollow bones and a covering of feathers. The feathers give a bird's wing its aerofoil shape (see page 3). Like flying insects, birds manage to overcome gravity by using their wings to push against the air and propel themselves upwards and forwards.

These photographs of a barn owl pouncing on a mouse show how the owl moves its wings.

The first feather

The first feather known to have existed was found in a **fossil**. It belonged to a half-bird, half-lizard, called an Archaeopteryx, that lived about 150 million years ago.

This picture shows a model of Archaeopteryx, as scientists believe it might have looked.

This barn owl relies on silent flight to hunt at night.

A flapping monster

Firmin Bousson's flying machine, built in 1900, tried, unsuccessfully, to imitate the flapping of a bird's wings.

Did you know?

Each year, seabirds called Arctic terns fly from the Arctic to the Antarctic and back again – a distance of 35,000 km!

In a flap

As the robin's wings are pushed downwards and backwards, the feathers are spread to create a bigger surface area, and give greater power. On the upbeat, they are separated and twisted so that air flows between them.

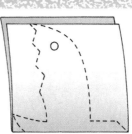

Feathers

As well as being used for flight, feathers keep a bird warm and waterproof.

A small bird has over 1000 feathers, a duck has 12,000 and a swan has 25,000.

Flight experiment

THE ONE-FLAP WONDER

You need

- 15 × 10cm piece of stiff card
- Small, thin elastic band
- Two used matchsticks
- Sticky tape
- Scissors

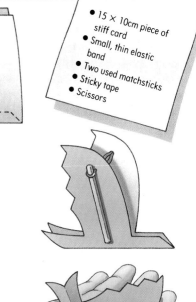

1 Fold the card in half. Draw half a bird on one side, with its body on the fold.

2 Cut out the bird. With paper still folded, cut out two holes through the wings. The distance from the holes to the fold should be about the same length as the elastic band.

3 Thread the elastic band through the wing holes. Push matchsticks into the loops at each end of it. Use sticky tape to fix the matches to the wings.

Straighten out the bird's wings and let it rest on the palm of your hand. Curl your fingers slightly to support its wingtips. Straighten your fingers gradually. Suddenly the bird will flap off. The elastic band works like the bird's wing muscles.

Skinny wings

Bats are the only **mammals** that can fly by flapping their wings like birds. But bats do not have feathers. Their wings are made of skin, stretched over thin finger bones.

The **skeleton** of a bat's wing is shaped rather like a human hand. The thumb is hooked and is used to clamber around the bat **roost**. It is also used as a comb, for a quick wash and brush-up.

Bats cannot fly as far as birds, but their broad wings allow them to swerve and dodge while they chase after insects.

Flying among the dinosaurs

Pterodactyls flew around dinosaur-infested swamps over 65 million years ago. Some had a wingspan of up to 8 metres. They did not have strong flight muscles and probably could do little more than glide.

Hanging in the air

A hang-glider has an aluminium frame, strong and light rather like a bat's skeleton, and a nylon sail like a bat's skin.

A hang-glider cannot flap its wings like a bat, and has to rely on air currents to keep it airborne.

Going batty!

A bat's legs are attached to the back of its wings, which means that they create a large area of stretched skin for flying. However, this means that it is difficult for it to walk or perch. Instead, when a bat wants to rest, it hangs upside down.

Flight experiment

BAT KITE

You need
- Piece of black or grey paper 15cm × 20cm
- Piece of paper 5cm square
- Scissors
- Sticky tape
- 3 long drinking straws
- Strong cotton thread

1 Cut semi-circles from two short edges and one long edge of the 15cm × 20cm piece of paper.

2 Cut one straw to a length of 20cm. Roll the uncut edge of the paper around the straw. Fasten with sticky tape.

3 Join the other two straws end to end with tape. Fix them to make a T-shape with the first straw. Bend the 20 cm straw to make a shallow V-shape.

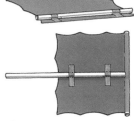

4 Fold the 5 cm-square paper into a fan. Tape it to the tail end.

5 Stick 18 cm of cotton to points A and B on the underside of the kite.

6 Tie a long length of cotton to this loop. Your bat kite will fly in very light winds.

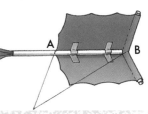

17

Taking off

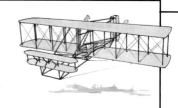

Take-off can be tricky for planes and for big birds. They have to build up enough speed on the ground to create the lift that will get them into the air. It takes time for a big bird or aeroplane to **accelerate** (speed up) enough so it can fly. Little birds can accelerate much more quickly and are in the air with a jump and a flap.

Prepare for take-off...

It seems unlikely that a plane roaring down a runway will ever leave the ground. But it does! A heavy jet has to travel at 200–300 km/h before enough lift is created by the air rushing past its wings to support the weight of the plane.

Planes, like birds, find it easier to take off 'into', or facing, the wind, as this increases the flow of air over the wings.

Pigeon take-off

Birds like this pigeon do not need a runway; they can take off vertically. During take-off the wing feathers are spread to catch more air and create more lift. The wings are raised and lowered so far that you can hear them clapping together.

Instant take-off

Because this coal tit is so light, it finds it easy to take off, and can do so in a split second whenever it senses danger. It uses its powerful legs to push itself off and with a strong downbeat of its wings is away, turning in mid-air as it goes.

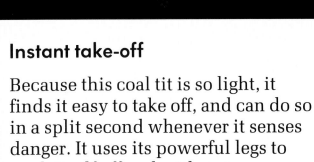

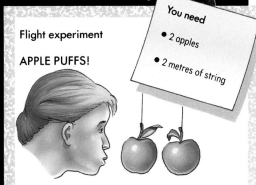

Walking on water

Large birds, such as swans and these flamingoes, take off rather like aeroplanes. They turn into the wind and run across the water, flapping their wings until they eventually struggle into the air.

Flight experiment

APPLE PUFFS!

You need
- 2 apples
- 2 metres of string

1 Tie a metre of string to each apple and hang them up so they are about 5cm apart.

2 Blow hard between the two apples. What happens?

The apples are drawn together. This is because of the change in air pressure. When you blow, you move the air *between* the apples and so reduce its pressure. The air pressure either side of the apples stays high and this pushes the apples inwards. Differences in air pressure enable planes to take off and remain in the air.

Landing

Birds, aeroplanes, bats and bees have to slow down in order to avoid crash landings. Many birds stop flapping their wings and glide to slow down. Just before touchdown they raise their head and chest and spread their wings and tail feathers. This increases their air resistance so that the bird stops flying and drops neatly on to its feet.

Birds face into the wind in order to land safely; they use the force of the wind blowing against them to help them slow down. Aircraft do the same whenever possible, although they may have to land with the wind blowing across them, depending on the direction of the runway.

Coming in to land

When an aeroplane comes in to land, the pilot slows the engines. Wing flaps are extended out of the back of the wings to increase air resistance and maintain lift at the slower speed. When the plane is just above the runway the pilot raises its nose slightly and slows the engines again. Because air is no longer flowing fast over the wings, there is not enough lift to keep the plane in the air and it lands on the ground.

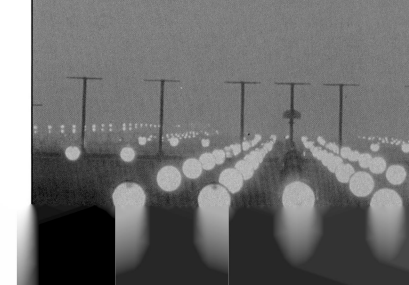

Gannets

This gannet is just about to land. The front edges of its wings are tilted upwards and its tail is fanned out. This helps to slow it down.

Blue tits

Blue tits are aerial acrobats. They are such good fliers that they can even land upside down inside a half coconut shell.

Small birds do not have the same landing problems as big, heavy birds. They are very light and have large wings for their body size. This means that they can brake very quickly.

Did you know?

The albatross is the largest seabird in the world. It uses its huge feet as airbrakes to help it land.

Flight experiment

DOWN TO EARTH

How do birds come in to land? If you have a garden or local park, watch how different kinds of birds behave as they land.

Things to watch for:

How they use their wings. Do they beat faster or slower as they come in to land?

Do they slow down? How?

How do they use their feet?

What happens if there is a strong wind?

You need

- Powers of observation
- Binoculars, if you have some

Hovering

Forward flight uses the action of moving through the air to create lift. Staying still in the air (**hovering**) uses much more energy, as a bird or insect has to beat its wings very fast to create enough lift to stay in the air.

Many insects are able to hover, but only a few birds can. Hummingbirds hover over flowers to feed on nectar. Kestrels and other birds of **prey** hover so that their eyes can detect the movement of small animals on the ground.

Hoverfly magic

You can see hoverflies in hot weather. Watch one hovering in front of a flower. Its wings beat more than 500 times a second, but they move up and down so little they hardly seem to move at all.

Did you know?

Hummingbirds beat their wings up to 80 times each second.

A kestrel's eye view

A hovering kestrel flies into the wind at exactly the right speed so that it moves neither forwards nor backwards.

Damselflies

Damselflies are the helicopters of the insect world. Their wings act rather like the helicopter's rotor. The front pair of wings moves out of step with the back pair, which means that the damselfly can hover.

How a helicopter works

Helicopters have rotors on top instead of wings. The rotor is like a moving wing. It lifts a helicopter off the ground and makes it hover. The little tail rotor stops the helicopter from spinning around.

Flight experiment

IN A SPIN!

Make your own rotor out of paper, powered by your breath!

1 Find the centre of the piece of paper by drawing diagonal lines from corner to corner. Where the lines cross is the centre.

2 Cut along the lines with the scissors, *stopping 1 cm from the centre.*

3 Curl each corner over to the middle. Push a pin through all the corners and the centre of the paper.

4 Push the point of the pin into the eraser on the end of the pencil.

5 Blow gently on the paper to make the spinner spin. Which part do you need to blow on to make it spin best?

You need

- A square piece of paper
- A pencil with an eraser on the end
- A ruler
- A pin
- Scissors

Fold

Fold

Paper

Pencil

Speeding

What have swallows, swifts and housemartins in common with space rockets? The answer is **streamlining**.

To travel at high speed through the air an animal or object must be smooth and slim so that the air flows past easily and there is the minimum of air resistance. A rocket is streamlined because it has to travel extremely fast through the air before it gets into space. Once in space there is no air resistance, so satellites, space telescopes and moon landers do not need to be streamlined.

Cockchafer

Beetles like this cockchafer are far too chunky to fly fast. They are not streamlined. The fastest insect fliers are long thin dragonflies, some of which can fly at 58 km/h in short bursts.

This is the Apollo 11 rocket, which was launched in 1969. It carried the astronauts who first landed on the Moon.

Flight experiment

STREAMLINING

Make a model windmill and use it to study streamlining.

1 Tape the straws together at the middle to form a cross.

2 Fold the card in half and cut into four equal pieces.

3 Tape the V-shaped pieces of card to the ends of the straws, making sure the Vs all face in the same direction.

4 Push the pin through the centre of the straws and into the top of the pencil. The windmill should spin when you hold it in the wind.

5 Does the wheel always turn in the same direction, whichever way the wind blows?

The wheel will always turn in the same direction no matter which side the wind blows. This is because the V-shaped pieces are streamlined in one direction and trap the wind in the other.

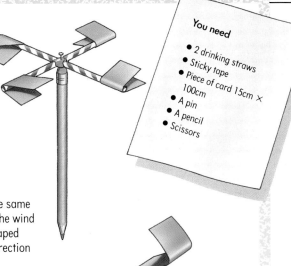

You need
- 2 drinking straws
- Sticky tape
- Piece of card 15cm × 100cm
- A pin
- A pencil
- Scissors

Speed merchants

Swallows, swifts and housemartins are all fast-flying birds. This swallow has streamlined curved wings and uses its speedy flying skills to catch insects. Swifts are the fastest, spending much of their lives speed-flying at 100 km/h or more.

Did you know?

The Asian swift is the fastest bird in the world. It can reach speeds of 170 km/h and fly 900 km a day.

Small birds

Some birds are so small and light that air resistance acts as a brake. They solve this problem by first flapping their wings and then folding them against their streamlined bodies.

Lighter than air

You don't always need wings to fly! Balloons lift off the ground because they are lighter than air.

Air itself can be made lighter by heating it up. So, if you fill a balloon with hot air it will float upwards. This is how the enormous hot-air balloons below are able to fly. They have to be huge, otherwise they could not lift the basket with the people inside.

There are some gases that are lighter than air. They can all be used to fill balloons, but helium is the safest because it will not burn.

Fire power

Heating up the air inside a huge balloon causes it to rise into the air. But for the balloon to stay up, the air has to be kept warm by means of a flame from a gas burner. If the air is allowed to cool, it gets heavier and the balloon sinks.

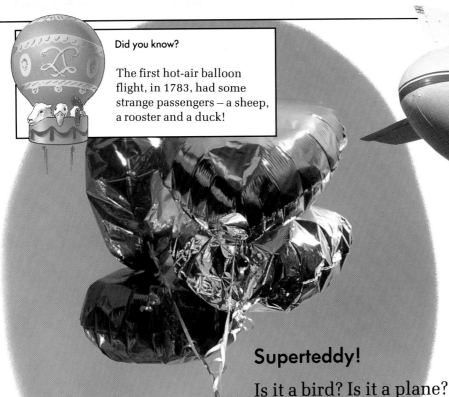
Superteddy!

Is it a bird? Is it a plane? No, it's a flying teddy! Three helium balloons can carry a small teddy up, up and away.

Airships

The first airships were filled with hydrogen and powered by steam engines. This was very dangerous, as the hydrogen could catch fire. Today, airships are filled with helium, which is much safer.

Soap bubble

A soap bubble consists of a thin layer of soapy water, filled with air. If blown with warm air outdoors on a cold day, the bubble will rise until the air inside it cools.

Flight experiment

HOT AIR BUBBLES

You need
- Plastic yogurt pot
- Shallow dish or saucer
- Washing-up liquid
- Scissors

1 Cut a hole 1-2cm across in the bottom of the yogurt pot, using the scissors.

2 Put a squirt of washing-up liquid into the saucer. Add about five times as much water, and stir.

3 Dip the open end of the yogurt pot into the soapy mixture and then blow through the hole to make a big bubble. It can be released by moving the pot sideways.

Try blowing bubbles indoors, then try again outside. If it is a cold day, watch how your warm breath makes the bubbles rise. The bigger and thinner the bubbles, the higher they go!

Blow into hole

Thermals and upcurrents

On hot, still, sunny days, some areas of the ground get hotter than others. They cause rising currents of hot air called **thermals**.

Rising air currents – known as **upcurrents** – are also caused when wind blows against a cliff or hillside and is forced upwards.

Thermals and upcurrents are used by birds and hang-gliders to enable them to stay in the air without effort.

White pelicans

These white pelicans are using their large wings to trap rising air. **Soaring** like this, they can fly for hours, using little energy but covering long distances.

Dust devils!

When warm air rises it can form spirals of air which suck up dust, leaves and litter. These **whirlwinds** are known as 'dust devils'.

SNAKES ALIVE!

See how warm air rises.

You need
- A pencil
- A piece of card
- An empty cotton reel
- Scissors
- A pencil with an eraser on the end
- A thimble

1 Draw a spiral snake on the piece of card. It must be wide enough so the hole in the middle will fit snugly over the thimble. Cut the snake out.

2 Make a stand for the snake. Put the pointed end of the pencil into the cotton reel. Put a pin in the eraser at the other end of the pencil and balance the thimble on the pin.

3 Slip the hole in the snake's tail over the thimble.

4 Put the snake over a warm radiator. As the warm air rises the snake will start to turn.

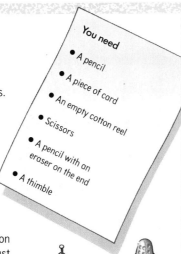

Hang-gliders

Hang-gliders soar like a bird, using upcurrents created by wind blowing against a hillside or cliff.

Gliders

Gliders have no engines. They use thermals to soar silently through the air. They are made of very lightweight material and have extra long wings to give them extra lift.

Propellers and jets

Aeroplanes are powered by **propellers** or jet engines.

A propeller is like a rotating wing. It pulls an aeroplane forwards through the air.

A jet engine runs on hot gas. Air is sucked in at the front of the engine, is mixed with fuel and burnt to produce hot gases that are forced rapidly out of the rear of the engine. This pushes the plane forward.

Propellers used to be carved out of many layers of wood glued together. Now they are made of light metal.

Nature's propellers

Some seeds, such as the ones shown here, have their own propeller blades. The wind catches in these propellers as the seeds fall from the tree. The spinning propellers then carry the seeds away from the parent tree so that they can find their own space in which to grow.

Seeds from a lime tree attached to a 'propeller'.

The spinning action of a Norway maple seed, caught in the wind.

Plane propellers

An aeroplane's propeller is shaped in such a way that, when it spins, air is drawn from in front and pushed out behind. This pushes the plane forward.

An amazing water rocket

This experimental rocket is water powered. It is made from a plastic bottle, part-filled with water. Air is pumped in until the pressure builds up to such a level that the bung in the neck is blown out . . . and up the rocket goes, leaving a stream of water.

Jet engines

Most large modern planes are powered by jet engines – one, or sometimes two, on each wing.

A jet plane can fly faster than any propeller-driven one. The fastest jet-powered passenger plane is Concorde, which reaches speeds of over 2300 km/h.

Did you know?

A few sea creatures, such as octopus and squid, use jet propulsion. They squirt out water at high speed to propel themselves through the water.

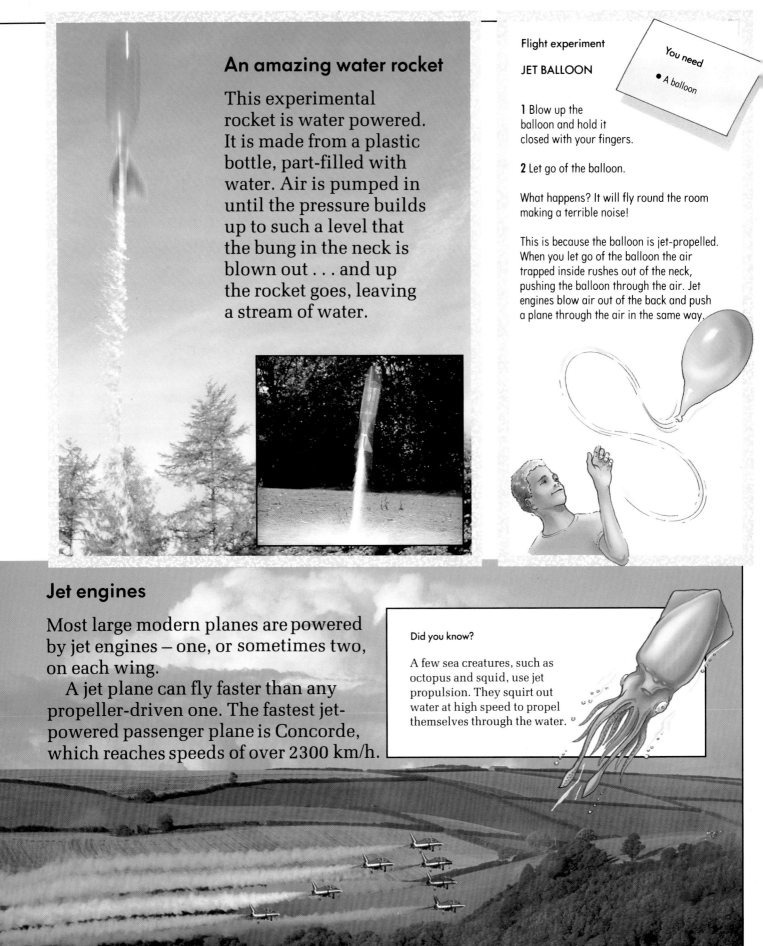

Flying words

Accelerate To speed up.

Aerofoil The special shape of an aeroplane's wing that enables it to lift off the ground.

Air pressure The squeezing effect of air caused by its weight.

Air resistance The slowing effect created by the force of air pushing against anything moving through it.

Fossil The remains of an animal or plant that existed many millions of years ago, or its imprint in rock.

Gravity A force that pulls everything towards the centre of the Earth.

Hovering Remaining in one place in the air.

Jet engine An engine that propels a plane or boat forwards by forcing air and gas out backwards under pressure.

Lift The upward force created by the flow of air over a wing.

Mammal Any type of warm-blooded animal that gives birth to babies and feeds them on its own milk.

Nectar A sugary liquid produced by flowers.

Parachute A canopy that catches the wind, allowing the object attached to it to drop slowly through the air.

Predator A creature that hunts other animals for food.

Prey An animal that is hunted and eaten by other creatures.

Propeller A blade that spins in air or water, propelling an aeroplane or boat forward.

Roost A place where bats or birds sleep or rest.

Rotor Anything that is spun around. A propeller is a kind of rotor. Helicopters have rotor blades.

Skeleton The bones that form the framework of the body.

Soaring Gliding on upward-moving air.

Streamlined Shaped so as to present the least possible air resistance.

Thermals Currents of warm, rising air.

Upcurrents Upward-moving air caused by wind meeting a hillside or cliff.

Whirlwind A spiralling wind.

Wingspan The distance from one wing tip to the other of a bird or aircraft.

Index

PICTURE CREDITS

All photographs are by Kim Taylor and Jane Burton except for those supplied by Allsport 29 *bottom*; Bruce Coleman 10 *lower left*, 11 *top*, 28 *left*; Mary Evans, 14 *black and white*; Eye Ubiquitous 3, 5 *bottom*, 31 *bottom*; Oxford Scientific Films 5 *top*; TRH 18 *bottom*; Zefa 4 *top*, 6 *top*, 8 *top*, 9 *bottom*, 10 *lower right*, 11 *bottom*, 16 *bottom*, 20-21, 23 *bottom*, 24 *main picture*, 26 *both pictures*, 27 *top right*, 29 *top*, 30 *lower right*.